THE EGYPTIAN NEWS

Author: SCOTT STEEDMAN ◆ Consultant: JAMES PUTNAM

Dear Reader,

Here at THE EGYPTIAN NEWS, we've been celebrating more than 3,000 years of our civilization's history.

We've hunted through past copies of our newspaper to find the stories that really made the headlines — and here they are, specially rewritten for this collector's edition.

Along with news stories on the great events that shaped our history, you'll find fascinating features on everyday life — from a revealing interview with a royal embalmer to advice on choosing the perfect pet and how to behave at the party of a lifetime.

We've had a great time putting this edition of THE EGYPTIAN NEWS together. We hope you have just as much fun reading it!

Chief Scribe

A NOTE FROM OUR PUBLISHER

As we all know, the ancient Egyptians didn't really have newspapers.
But if they had, we're sure they would all have been reading *The Egyptian News*!
We hope you enjoy it.

Gareth Stevens Publishing
A WORLD ALMANAC EDUCATION GROUP COMPANY

THE NEWS

LIFESTYLE

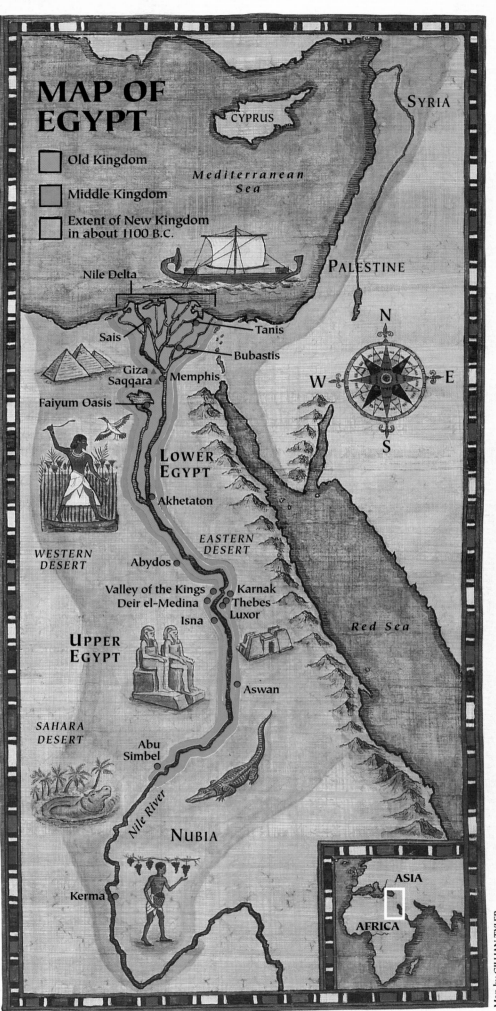

MAP OF EGYPT

- ☐ Old Kingdom
- ☐ Middle Kingdom
- ☐ Extent of New Kingdom in about 1100 B.C.

CYPRUS

SYRIA

Mediterranean Sea

PALESTINE

Nile Delta

Sais

Tanis

Bubastis

Giza
Saqqara
Memphis

Faiyum Oasis

N
W   E
S

LOWER EGYPT

Akhetaton

EASTERN DESERT

WESTERN DESERT

Abydos

Valley of the Kings
Deir el-Medina

Karnak
Thebes
Luxor

Isna

Red Sea

UPPER EGYPT

Aswan

SAHARA DESERT

Abu Simbel

Nile River

NUBIA

Kerma

ASIA

AFRICA

Map by GILLIAN TYLER

SOARING SUCCESS!

Illustrated by CHRIS FORSEY

STEP BY STEP: Surrounded by fan bearers, Pharaoh Zoser visits his completed tomb.

THE PYRAMIDS ARE now such a familiar sight that it's almost impossible to imagine our country without them. Yet when the first pyramid was built as a tomb for Pharaoh Zoser in 2680 B.C., it was a startlingly new idea.

BUT WHOSE idea was it? To search for the answer *The Egyptian News* looked back down the centuries to the time when this tomb was built — at the beginning of Egypt's first great period, now known as the Old Kingdom.

Very few records exist from this time, and facts are hard to come by. We do know, however, that before 2680 B.C. all our pharaohs were buried in mastaba tombs.

So why did Zoser decide against these low mud-brick buildings in favor of a more costly and complicated design? Many people believe that the pharaoh was influenced by his royal architect, Imhotep, who must have convinced him that a pyramid of stone steps would act as a stairway to the gods.

PYRAMID GROWS

In any event, it seems likely that when the pharaoh first agreed to the project, he had little idea just how massive his finished tomb was going to be!

Imhotep changed his plans five times during the tomb's construction. And with each change, the pyramid grew bigger.

By the time it was finished he had created an incredible structure of solid stone, six tiers high, which towered 200 feet above the desert sands at Saqqara.

Beneath the pyramid there was a network of narrow passages. These led down to the burial chambers, where Zoser and his family were eventually laid to rest.

The Step Pyramid, as it later became known, was a truly magnificent achievement. And, as we are all aware, the idea quickly caught on.

Over the next 1,000 years, every pharaoh who could afford one wanted a pyramid to be built as his final resting place. 𓀀

On pages 20–21 we take a close look at the greatest pyramid of all and ask when and why pyramid tombs went out of fashion....

EGYPT REUNITED

Illustrated by ANGUS M^cBRIDE

IN 2040 B.C., a young prince called Mentuhotep was crowned Lord of Two Lands. For the first time in over 100 years, the whole of Egypt was united under one ruler. *The Egyptian News* examines the events that led up to this great occasion.

THE PEACEFUL years of the Old Kingdom were over by 2160 B.C. A series of weak pharaohs had lost control of our country and it had become divided into two lands — Upper Egypt and Lower Egypt.

Civil war broke out as ambitious local rulers gathered together armies and fought one another for the throne. But none of them succeeded, and the war dragged on year after year.

Matters were made even worse when foreign armies invaded Lower Egypt from the north-east, trying to claim parts of the country for themselves. Our glorious civilization was rapidly falling apart!

A PRINCE OF THEBES

Then a prince from the southern city of Thebes led an army north to battle against the foreign invaders. His name was Mentuhotep.

Guided by his skill and great courage, the prince's army drove the invaders out of Egypt.

Mentuhotep now set out to win the throne. With the strength of his

BATTLE GLORY: Mentuhotep's men prove their courage against the invading armies.

victorious army behind him, he soon defeated his rivals. And in 2040 B.C., he gained control of both Upper and Lower Egypt. With a huge sense of relief, the whole country welcomed him as their new pharaoh.

Mentuhotep's rule was a time of prosperity and peace for our people.

Not only did this mighty pharaoh stay in power for 50 years, but his reign gave rise to our second great age, the Middle Kingdom.

HISTORY REPEATS ITSELF

THIS WAS NOT the first time in its long and eventful past that our country had been divided.

AT THE VERY beginning of our history, Upper and Lower Egypt were ruled separately. Each had its own king.

Then, in 3150 B.C., came the legendary ruler who first reigned over the whole of Egypt — the first man to take the title Lord of Two Lands.

Sadly, this great man lived so long ago that many facts about him have been lost, including his true name. But one thing that we know for sure is that he was the first to wear the double crown — combining the white crown of Upper Egypt with the red crown of Lower Egypt.

Since that time, the double crown has come to represent not only the union of our two lands, but also the supreme authority of the pharaoh who rules over us all.

Map by SIMONE BONI

LOWER EGYPT

•Thebes

UPPER EGYPT

Nile River

TWO LANDS — one country.

Illustrated by TONY SMITH

TWO CROWNS — in one.

HYKSOS HAMMERED

THE PEACE AND PROSPERITY of the Middle Kingdom came to a sorry end in 1786 B.C., when Egypt was once more torn in two — this time by the Hyksos.

THESE "ASIATICS" from Palestine migrated into northern Egypt, looting and burning everything in their path. It wasn't long before they took over the whole of Lower Egypt, and for over 200 years, our people were under their rule.

Then, in the 1560s B.C., Sekenenra, the king of Upper Egypt, attempted to drive the Hyksos out. But before he could do so, he was seriously wounded in battle and later died. His successor to the throne, Kamose, then took up the fight.

THE BATTLE CONTINUES

Year after year the war raged, until slowly the tide began to turn and the Hyksos were forced to retreat northward.

After one of his many victories, Kamose proudly claimed, "I was on the enemy like a falcon, I brought down his walls, I massacred his men. . . . My soldiers were like lions with their prey."

Disaster struck when Kamose was killed on the battlefield. The crown of Upper Egypt now passed to Ahmose, Kamose's brother.

Bent on revenge, the young king immediately marched north to join his men. Inspired by its new leader, the army fought with fresh courage.

And in the 1550s B.C., the Hyksos capital, Tanis, fell and the invaders fled.

HYKSOS GO HOME

Ahmose now chased the Hyksos all the way back to Palestine. Only when he knew that our country was safe did he return to Thebes to be crowned pharaoh of all Egypt.

And with a strong ruler back on the throne, Egypt saw the dawn of a glorious new age — the New Kingdom. 𓅓

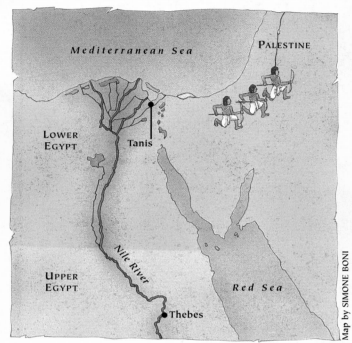
Map by SIMONE BONI

ON THE RUN! The Hyksos are chased back to Palestine.

FIGHTING FIT: The new Egyptian soldier.

FEARSOME FORCE

Illustrated by CHRISTIAN HOOK

ALL EGYPT CELEBRATED when the Hyksos were driven from our land. But without these invaders, our army would never have become the fearsome force it is today.

FOR CENTURIES Egypt had relied on small local armies, supported by ordinary citizens in times of war. But our untrained troops were no match for the skills of the Hyksos.

With their superior weapons and tactics, the conquest of Lower Egypt was all too easy for these foreign warriors.

The only way our troops could hope to defeat the Hyksos was by learning from them!

So for the first time, Egypt began to build its own professional army. Horses and war chariots,

along with armor and curved swords, were all copied from the enemy — and used against them with great success.

Today our troops pride themselves on their battle skills, whether they fight on foot, from chariots, or even from ships.

And with the strength of these highly trained soldiers behind them, our pharaohs have not only kept our borders safe, but conquered new lands to build the mighty empire we control today. 𓅓

QUEEN ROCKS NATION

Illustrated by JAMES PUTNAM

IN 1479 B.C., A QUEEN shocked the nation by declaring herself Lord of Two Lands. *The Egyptian News* **looks at the career of our country's most famous female pharaoh.**

IT WAS NOT surprising that when Thutmose II died in 1479 B.C. his wife Hatshepsut was asked to rule in his place. After all, his son was barely more than a baby. And this wasn't the first time a queen had governed Egypt on behalf of a child.

But Hatshepsut wanted to do more than just rule in her stepson's name. So she took the dramatic step of calling herself pharaoh and Lord of Two Lands, instead.

What's more, she also took on the traditional symbols of a pharaoh — the double crown, the crook, the flail, and even the false beard!

WEAK WOMAN?

At the time, Hatshepsut's actions outraged many people, and the records describe her as a weak ruler because she did little to expand our empire.

But throughout her reign, the skills of our craftsmen and architects flourished.

She also sent out one of the greatest trading expeditions in our history. A large fleet of ships sailed to the land of Punt at the mouth of the Red Sea and returned with a

CAST OFF: Piled high with exotic goods, Hatshepsut's ships prepare for the long journey home from Punt.

CRAZY KING CAUSES CHAOS

CLOSED

Cartoon by TONY KENYON

EGYPT'S PRIESTS rejoiced at the death of Amenhotep IV in 1336 B.C. During his 16 years as pharaoh, he had made their lives miserable — and had turned our religion upside down!

ALL SEEMED well when Amenhotep IV first came to the throne in 1352 B.C. But soon after he was crowned, the pharaoh became obsessed with a little-known sun god named Aton.

To the horror and outrage of the priests, he refused to worship any of the traditional gods. And just six years later, the pharaoh changed his name to Akhenaton, in honor of his god, Aton.

To make matters even worse, he then moved our capital city from Thebes to a brand new city that he had built and named Akhetaton.

In fact, the pharaoh became so besotted with Aton that he neglected his duties as ruler, and the government quickly fell into chaos.

It wasn't long before rumors started flying around that perhaps the pharaoh was going mad. And these stories seemed to be confirmed when Akhenaton sent out his soldiers to destroy every

Thutmose III, did not gain the throne until her death in 1457 B.C. By this time, Thutmose had developed such a deep hatred for Hatshepsut for keeping him from power that he had her name removed from every monument.

However, it is clear to us now that during her reign, Hatshepsut ruled Egypt fairly and firmly. And here at *The Egyptian News*, we think it's time to restore her name to fame! 🖾

fortune in copper, ivory, and incense trees.

In fact, far from being a weak ruler, Hatshepsut's grip on her kingdom was so strong that her stepson,

BOY-KING DIES

Illustrated by TONY SMITH

WHEN TUTANKHAMEN died in 1327 B.C., he was only 17 years old. *The Egyptian News* **investigates the mysterious events that took place at the time of the pharaoh's sudden death.**

THE ROYAL embalmer who prepared the young pharaoh's body for the funeral said at the time that the skull appeared to have been damaged.

But the high priest, Ay, refused to set up an inquiry into the boy's death. A funeral was hastily arranged, and the pharaoh was buried in a rock tomb in the Valley of the Kings.

The treasures sealed inside Tutankhamen's tomb were rumored to be stunning — priceless

jewelry, statues, and furniture, as well as three glittering coffins, the innermost made of solid gold.

In fact, it was a very extravagant funeral for a pharaoh who had ruled for just nine years.

Throughout most of Tutankhamen's reign, the real rulers were Ay and the commander of the army, Horemheb.

But as Tutankhamen grew older, he became less easy for the two men to control.

The possibility that the pharaoh might be about to challenge their position, and take over the running of the country himself, must have horrified both Ay and Horemheb.

But would either of these men have been desperate enough to kill Tutankhamen? Both of them certainly gained from the boy's death, for afterward, first Ay and then Horemheb was crowned pharaoh.

Sadly, the truth may never be known — it lies buried with Tutankhamen! 🖾

---

image they could find of our other gods and to close down their temples. Thousands of priests lost their jobs.

ALONE ON THE THRONE

When Akhenaton died in 1336 B.C., he left behind a brokenhearted widow, Nefertiti, and an 8-year-old son, Tutankhaton.

Within three years, Nefertiti had also died, leaving Tutankhaton to rule Egypt on his own.

With an 11-year-old boy now on the throne,

the priests wasted no time in restoring the old gods and reopening their temples. One of the high priests, Ay, seized control of the government and ruled the country in Tutankhaton's name.

The city of Akhetaton was abandoned, and the young Tutankhaton was taken back to the old capital of Thebes.

And then, as a last gesture to rid Egypt of the unhappy memory of Akhenaton and his god, the high priests renamed the boy-king Tutankhamen. 🖾

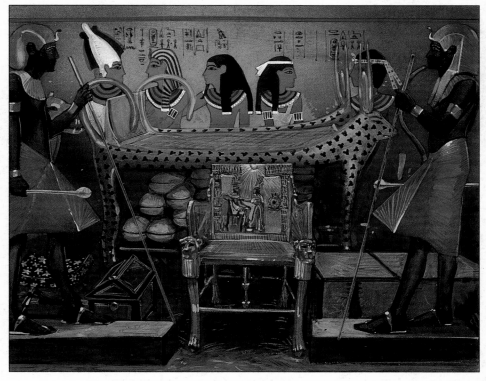

GUILTY GOLD? Just some of the priceless objects buried with Tutankhamen.

THE FINAL FAREWELL

Illustrated by NICK HARRIS

IN 1213 B.C., ALL EGYPT mourned the loss of Ramses the Great — a remarkable pharaoh who had ruled us for 66 years. A reporter from *The Egyptian News* was at the funeral.

THIS MORNING I stood on the East Bank of the Nile at Thebes, where 70 days ago crowds of sobbing people were gathered. They had come to see the funeral boat of Ramses II carry his body across the river to the West Bank, where it was to be embalmed.

The crowds were out again today, this time to watch as the royal family sailed across the Nile to lead the pharaoh's funeral procession.

By the time I joined the mourners on the West Bank, the procession was already under way.

The mummified body of the pharaoh lay inside a richly decorated coffin, which had been placed on a golden sledge for its long journey to the funerary temple.

As the sledge moved away, the mourners were led by Ramses' 13th son, Merneptah, our new pharaoh. He was followed by the other members of the royal family.

Behind them walked a number of government officials and a group of priests chanting sacred songs. Then came the professional mourners, wailing and throwing dust into the air.

Last of all, there was a long line of attendants, carrying the many things Ramses will need when he reaches the next world, the Afterlife.

Along with all of his personal belongings were rich presents of jewelry and furniture, as well as hundreds of shabti — clay models of the servants that will care for him in the Afterlife.

After many hours the long procession reached the funerary temple. At this point the mourners were left behind, as the priests took the coffin into the temple to carry out the final stages of the funeral.

EYEWITNESS EXCLUSIVE

An eyewitness, who asked not to be named, told me what happened next.

Inside the temple, he watched as the priests performed the Opening of the Mouth ceremony that will allow the pharaoh to speak in the Afterlife.

Then, Ramses' coffin was carried to a hidden tomb cut deep into the rocks in the Valley of the Kings.

The coffin was taken to the burial chamber far inside the tomb, where it was enclosed in a stone sarcophagus.

Silently the priests left, and the tomb was sealed forever.

REST IN THE WEST: The funeral procession makes its way to Ramses II's temple on the West Bank of the Nile.

MURDER FOILED!

Illustrated by PETER DENNIS

Illustrated by MIKE WHITE

RAMSES II, THE FACTS

❂ Ramses II is the only pharaoh in our long history to have the title "the Great" added to his name.

❂ He was born in 1299 B.C. and came to the throne in 1279 B.C.

❂ At the Battle of Qadesh, in year 4 of his reign, he led an army against a massive Hittite force of over 40,000 men.

❂ In year 21 of his reign, Ramses and the Hittites signed a peace treaty that was to last until Ramses' death.

❂ Ramses II was responsible for the construction of more temples than any other pharaoh.

❂ Ramses II had an incredible number of children — 96 sons and 60 daughters!

❂ He died in 1213 B.C. at the age of 86.

❂ In memory of him, no fewer than nine other pharaohs took his name when they were crowned.

GUILTY! Queen Teye and her son, Pentaware, are arrested by the palace guards for attempted murder.

AS FAR AS *The Egyptian News* can discover, never in our history had a woman attempted to take the life of a pharaoh — never, that is, until the reign of Ramses III.

CROWNED IN the year 1184 B.C., Ramses III rapidly won fame as a wise ruler and a brave warrior. In the first ten years of his reign, this great pharaoh fought off no fewer than three invading foreign armies.

But incredibly, by the end of his rule, he was in far more danger in his own home than he had ever been in battle!

Like most of our pharaohs, Ramses III had a number of wives and many children. His troubles began when he refused to name one of his numerous sons as heir to the throne.

WICKED WIFE PLOTS MURDER

In 1152 B.C., one of Ramses' wives, Queen Teye, decided to take matters into her own hands. In a bid to put her son, Pentaware, on the throne, she hatched a dastardly plot.

Together with some of the other wives and a group of court officials, the queen set out to poison the pharaoh.

Fortunately, this evil attempt at murder failed, and Teye was arrested, along with her son and the other accomplices.

A special court of 12 judges was chosen to hear the case. But shockingly, five of the judges were discovered at a drunken party with the female traitors!

These foolish men were severely punished by having their noses and ears cut off.

New judges had to be found, and the trial was restarted. In the end, the traitors were found guilty and ordered to kill themselves. But first, to show the severity of the crime, their names were taken away by the court.

And as we know, this is the worst punishment anyone can suffer. For without a name, it is impossible for a soul to reach the Afterlife.

As for Ramses, it is likely that he never fully recovered from this vile attempt on his life — one year later he was dead.

And it seems as if our country never quite recovered either. For since that time, none of our pharaohs has ever been the equal of Ramses III — neither in wisdom nor in bravery.

WHO'S WHO?

Illustrated by MAXINE HAMIL

HOW MUCH do you know about the men who run our country? Do you know what the overseer of the granaries does, for example, or even your district governor? *The Egyptian News* gives you the facts.

OF COURSE, the most important person in the whole country is our great and glorious pharaoh, the Lord of Two Lands.

Never forget that as the son of the gods he is all-powerful. Everything in Egypt belongs to him — every field, every house, even every person.

But the pharaoh can't be expected to run our country on his own. So he is helped by the three next-most important men in the land — the Vizier of Upper Egypt, the Vizier of Lower Egypt, and the High Priest of Amon Ra.

By making sure that Amon Ra, the greatest of our gods, is honored properly, this high priest takes care of our country's most important religious needs. This leaves the two viziers to take care of our country's practical needs.

OVER TO THE OVERSEERS

To do this, the viziers are supported by a group of royal overseers, each one responsible for a particular area.

For example, there's the royal architect, the army commander, and the head of the law courts. There's also the overseer of irrigation — he's in charge of the ditches and channels that bring water to the fields. There's the overseer of the granaries, too, who makes sure that the farmers' grain harvests are properly recorded and stored.

And then there are the district governors! Did you know that there are 42 governors in all — one for each district, or nome? It is every governor's job to make sure that the day-to-day running of his nome is properly carried out.

Each district governor has a team of people to help him, of course, and, like all government officials, he has to be able to read and write. This is why every single government job, from the highest to the lowest, can go only to an educated man — a scribe.

But, at the end of the day, no matter how well organized our country is, its success relies on the support of its people. For it is the vast number of skilled craftsmen and hardworking farmers in Egypt that keeps our country great.

PYRAMID OF POWER: The many people whose labor supports our pharaoh.

PHARAOH

VIZIERS & THE HIGH PRIEST

ROYAL OVERSEERS

DISTRICT GOVERNORS

SCRIBES

CRAFTWORKERS

FARMERS

WRITE TO THE TOP

Illustrated by ANGUS McBRIDE

LET'S FACE IT, to get any kind of government job you have to be able to read and write. And you can become a scribe only if your father is one already. Born lucky? Perhaps, but scribes have to go to school — and that's just the beginning....

IT STARTS TOUGH and gets worse! The sons of craftsmen and farmers don't usually begin to learn their fathers' trades until they're 12 years old. So while these children are still playing with their toys, scribes' sons are already going to school — they start when they're only 5 years old.

ALL WORK AND NO PLAY

School teachers are very strict, and they really know how to make students work hard. Lazy boys are beaten or even expelled.

And there's a lot to remember, too. To begin with, the young scribes are taught how to read and write hieroglyphs — this means learning more than 700 of these picture symbols by heart.

Day after day, the boys use reed pens to copy hieroglyphs onto pieces of broken pottery. And only when they can do this perfectly are the students allowed to write on valuable papyrus.

By this time, they are also studying math, law, history, and geography. And really smart students are taught engineering and architecture, too.

School lasts seven

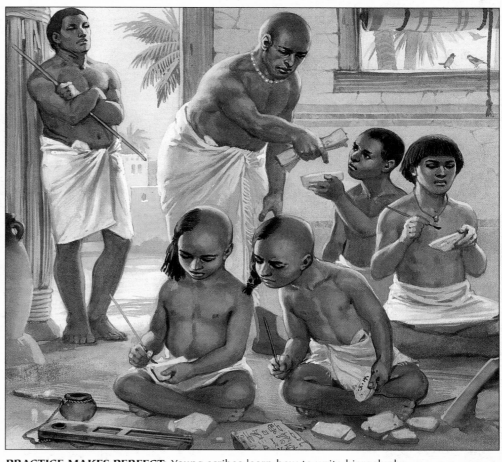

PRACTICE MAKES PERFECT: Young scribes learn how to write hieroglyphs.

years, which means that by the time they're 12, the boys are fully qualified scribes and have to go to work. And while there are plenty of jobs for them to do, few are easy or glamorous.

So the next time you wish you were a scribe, think again — being able to read and write isn't the easy route to power and riches that it may appear to be.

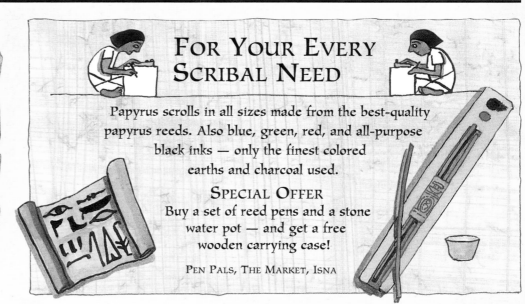

QUIT MOANING – PAY UP!

HERE AT *The Egyptian News,* we receive endless complaints from our readers about the amount of tax they have to pay to the government, either in goods or in work. But we think it's worth remembering just what our taxes are for.

WHO MAKES certain that our country has a strong army to defend it?

Who ensures that our families have grain to eat when the harvest fails?

Who gives our farmers the seeds to plant each year to grow their crops? And who makes sure that their fields are kept well supplied with water?

Who organizes the building of our glorious temples? And who hires the many priests we need to honor and serve the gods so that they will stay happy with us?

The answer to every one of these questions is, of course, our country's government.

But the government couldn't possibly accomplish all these things without our support. And that is why we have to pay taxes.

DON'T BE LAX, PAY YOUR TAX

Perhaps you're a scribe or a craftsman who pays tax by working for the pharaoh. Or maybe you're a farmer who pays in barley and wheat. No matter who you are, the time and goods that you give are invaluable. They supply the government with the means to keep our country strong and powerful.

So whenever you and your friends feel like moaning about the taxes you have to pay, just remember how important they are — and how much our country relies on you to provide them.

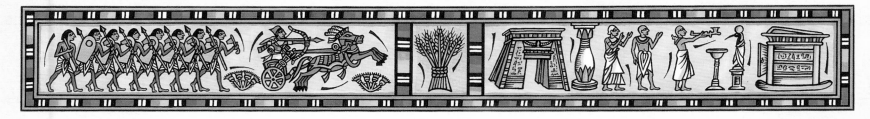

TAXING TALK

Illustrated by ROGER JONES

THIEVES, BULLIES, THUGS. Do our tax collectors really deserve such a bad reputation? *The Egyptian News* asked a tax scribe for his view.

I JUST DON'T understand why we tax scribes are so unpopular. I mean, we're only doing our job.

So the farmers have to give up a share of their crops to the pharaoh each year — what's the big deal? Their land belongs to the pharaoh anyway, so really all their crops are his, too. But some farmers still try to avoid paying what they owe.

Every year at the start of the growing season, I visit each farmer in my district. First, I measure his fields so I can work out the amount of grain he's likely to grow.

Then I calculate the value of his pigs, geese, goats, and cattle, and the produce he'll get from his fruit trees and vegetable plot. Only when I've done all this do I decide how much tax he'll be paying in wheat and barley.

Of course, the farmers don't make my job easy. They lie about how many animals they have or the size of their fields.

Some of them even try to bribe me. They think that if they give me a pig or some geese, I might charge them less tax. I ask you, is it worth losing my job over a pig?

And at harvesttime, when I return to collect the tax, it's the same thing all over again — lies, lies, and more lies. I tell you, these farmers just hate to pay up. That's why I always take a bodyguard with me. He makes them see straight!

PAY TIME: A tax scribe and his bodyguard come to collect.

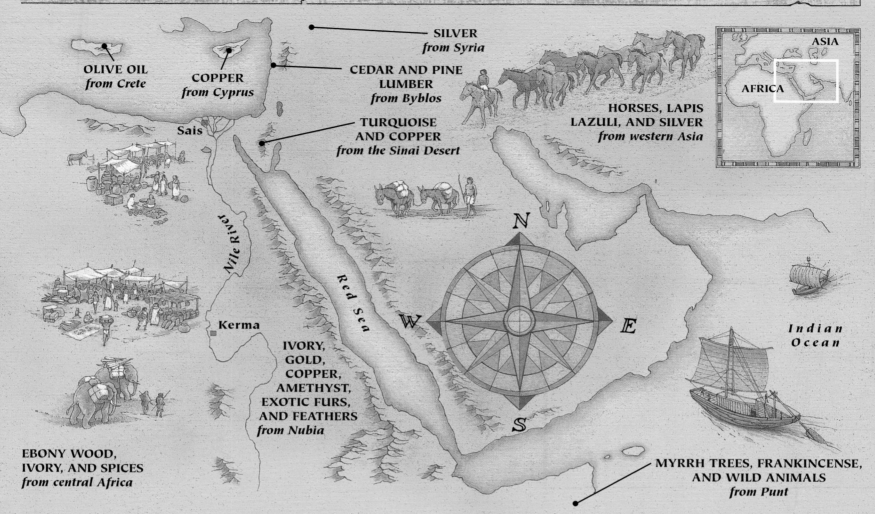

- **OLIVE OIL** *from Crete*
- **COPPER** *from Cyprus*
- Sais
- **SILVER** *from Syria*
- **CEDAR AND PINE LUMBER** *from Byblos*
- **TURQUOISE AND COPPER** *from the Sinai Desert*
- **HORSES, LAPIS LAZULI, AND SILVER** *from western Asia*
- ASIA
- AFRICA
- *Nile River*
- *Red Sea*
- N
- W
- E
- S
- **Kerma**
- *Indian Ocean*
- **IVORY, GOLD, COPPER, AMETHYST, EXOTIC FURS, AND FEATHERS** *from Nubia*
- **EBONY WOOD, IVORY, AND SPICES** *from central Africa*
- **MYRRH TREES, FRANKINCENSE, AND WILD ANIMALS** *from Punt*

THE WAY TO TRADE

Illustrated by PETER VISSCHER

HAVE YOU EVER thought about setting up a business as a trader? Discover the simplest route to success with *The Egyptian News*.

OF COURSE, the first thing you'll need is a sturdy boat, along with a crew of 20 to 30 men. They won't have much to do while you're sailing up the Nile, as the wind will push you along. But rowing downriver into the wind can be back-breaking work.

Load up your boat with cattle, grain, linen, papyrus, or high-quality building stone. All these goods are cheap in Egypt, since we have plenty of them. But outside our country's borders, they are worth their weight in gold — literally!

Now, where to trade? If you're really brave, you could set off for Cyprus or Syria. But the farther you travel, the greater the risk of dying abroad.

And if you were to die in some distant land, there'd be no one to give you a proper funeral, so you'd have no chance of reaching the Afterlife.

Instead, why not use a foreign merchant as a middleman? This means you won't have to travel any farther than one of our busy market towns, such as Kerma or Sais.

Here you'll find the middlemen who bring in all kinds of luxuries from other lands. And you can exchange your papyrus and grain for such exotic goods as Nubian ivory and Syrian silver.

You won't get wealthy overnight by staying so close to home, but at least you'll die happy! 🪲

LIFE ON THE RIVER

Illustrated by PETER DENNIS

FLOODS OF FORTUNE: Without the Nile we would be unable to grow our crops, and our country would become a lifeless desert.

IN A COUNTRY where it never rains, the annual flooding of the river Nile is essential to our whole civilization. But what does the Nile mean to the average Egyptian?

FARMER

Work, work, work. That's what the Nile means to me! The minute the flood season ends in October I'm working in the fields, plowing the rich black mud that the river has left behind. Once that's done, it's time to sow the wheat and barley seeds.

Next I have to open up the network of ditches crisscrossing the fields. Each ditch has gates linking it to one of the large channels cut into the banks of the Nile. And while the river level is still high enough, this system of channels and ditches brings water into the fields.

By March my crops are ready to harvest. But even when that's done, there's still more work to do.

Once the harvest is over, and the Nile is at its lowest, I have to repair any damage to the ditches and channels. They have to be in good condition by the time the next flood season starts in July, or I'll be in deep trouble. I tell you, the work is never-ending!

SCRIBE

I work for the overseer of irrigation, so the Nile is my responsibility. I check the river level every day on the nilometers — the measuring pillars that are sunk into the riverbed at regular points along the edge of the Nile.

If the water level hasn't started rising by July, we know it's going to be a hard year. If the fields aren't flooded by August, there won't be enough mud to enrich the soil. Our farmers won't be able to grow their crops, and we'll have to rely on the government to feed us.

FERRYMAN

I spend my life ferrying people up and down the Nile. It's the perfect way to get around! After all, there's no point building roads — they'd just get washed away in the flood. And anyway, who needs roads when you can go by boat from one end of the country to the other?

MOTHER

I love living by the river, but I do worry about my children. My husband has made them lucky fish charms to protect them from drowning. ⬛

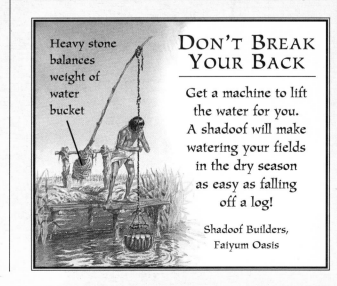

Heavy stone balances weight of water bucket

DON'T BREAK YOUR BACK

Get a machine to lift the water for you. A shadoof will make watering your fields in the dry season as easy as falling off a log!

Shadoof Builders, Faiyum Oasis

A GOOD IDEA OR SLAVE LABOR?

NOT ONLY do farmers have to hand over a share of their crops each year for taxes, but they also have to work on the pharaoh's building projects in the flood season. Is this fair? We asked two farmers for their opinion.

First farmer: I think the pharaoh has some nerve. Do *I* ask him to repair *my* house for nothing?

Second farmer: You can't speak about our pharaoh like that — you're talking about the son of the gods! If we help him by building his tomb and his temples, then surely the gods will look kindly on us.

First farmer: But if the work is so honorable, how come anyone with any power manages to get out of it? I haven't seen too many scribes or priests cutting stone in the quarries lately.

Second farmer: Well, it wouldn't be right, would

it? They've got far more important things to do.

And what about all those pyramids? You can't seriously be saying they weren't worth the effort.

First farmer: I bet the poor guys who hauled the stones didn't think so!

I still say that if the pharaoh wants a tomb or a temple built, he should let people decide for themselves if they want to help. I'd rather stay at home and repair my tools or sit in the shade and drink fig juice.

Second farmer: It's just as well most farmers aren't as selfish as you, then — if we didn't help the pharaoh, who would?

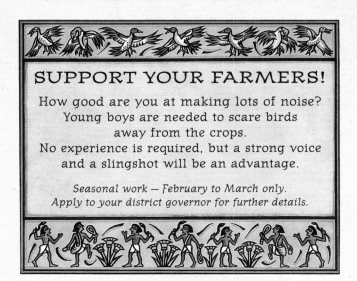

SUPPORT YOUR FARMERS!

How good are you at making lots of noise?
Young boys are needed to scare birds away from the crops.
No experience is required, but a strong voice and a slingshot will be an advantage.

Seasonal work — February to March only.
Apply to your district governor for further details.

BORED WITH BARTERING?

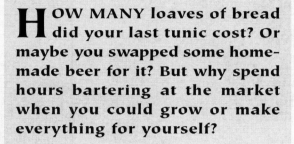

Illustrated by SUE HEAP

HOW MANY loaves of bread did your last tunic cost? Or maybe you swapped some home-made beer for it? But why spend hours bartering at the market when you could grow or make everything for yourself?

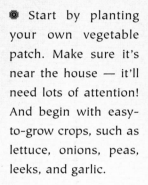

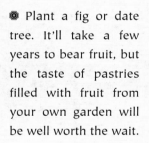

◎ Start by planting your own vegetable patch. Make sure it's near the house — it'll need lots of attention! And begin with easy-to-grow crops, such as lettuce, onions, peas, leeks, and garlic.

◎ Plant a fig or date tree. It'll take a few years to bear fruit, but the taste of pastries filled with fruit from your own garden will be well worth the wait.

◎ Be brave: keep bees! Not only will you get delicious honey from them, but you'll also be able to make candles from the beeswax.

◎ Spend a day in the marshes with a group of friends from your village. You can gather

reeds to make sandals, baskets, or floor mats, and maybe even catch some fish for supper.

◎ If you're handy on the loom, try growing flax plants. Then you can spin and weave linen cloth from the stems to make your family's clothes.

◎ Crush the oil from flax or sesame seeds. Use it to cook with, or create your own perfume by mixing it with flower petals.

◎ Getting tired of your favorite drink? Press the juice from fresh figs or dates to make a delicious and thirst-quenching drink!

BEHIND CLOSED DOORS

Illustrated by SIMONE BONI

ONLY THE PHARAOH and his priests are ever allowed into the heart of our temples. So when a reporter from *The Egyptian News* was invited to visit the magnificent temple of Amon Ra at Karnak, he couldn't believe his luck!

I MET MY guide outside the temple before dawn. He asked that his name remain secret, but he was proud to tell me that his title was God's Second Servant. This means that he is second only to the high priest of the temple — God's First Servant.

A CLOSE SHAVE AT THE TEMPLE

Before we could enter the temple we had to shave our heads and eyebrows. My guide told me that the priests do this every day to purify themselves for the god. Then, after bathing in the temple's sacred lake, we put on the leopard-skin robes worn by the priests.

Now we were ready to make our way into the temple. Soon we reached the grand hall — a vast chamber filled with rows of tall exquisitely painted columns.

The massive doors at the far end were hauled open, and we entered the holiest place in the entire temple, the inner chapel.

Inside it was cool and dark, and the air was sweet with incense burning to please the god.

My guide sprinkled our path with sacred lake water and chanted: "I am a Purified One."

As my eyes grew used to the darkness, I saw a gleaming shrine at the heart of the chapel. Then the shrine was opened, revealing a golden statue of Amon Ra.

Now the high priest leaned forward to touch

AWE-INSPIRING: Priests make their way through the grand hall to the inner chapel.

the statue, saying, "Awake in peace, Great God."

For the rest of the day, I watched as priests cared for the god's every need. They washed his statue and rubbed it with oils, before clothing it in fine linen garments. And every few hours a meal of wine, cakes, and fruit was laid before it.

Fortunately, Amon Ra was not the only one to eat. As each new offering was placed before his statue, the previous one

was taken to the priests' quarters, where we later sat down to a fine lunch.

By nightfall I was quite exhausted and relieved to leave the temple. But it had been a truly amazing experience, and one I'm proud to be able to share with our readers.

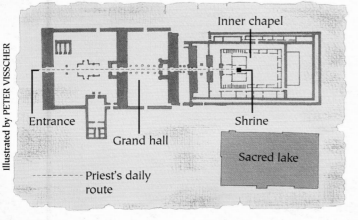

KARNAK: A plan of the main temple.

Inner chapel

Entrance

Grand hall

Shrine

Priest's daily route

Sacred lake

Illustrated by PETER VISSCHER

TOP GODS

Illustrated by TUDOR HUMPHRIES

WITH OVER 1,000 gods and goddesses, it's impossible to keep track of them all. Help is at hand, though, with our simple guide to the most important gods.

Ma'at, the goddess of truth and justice.

Amon Ra, the king of the gods and protector of the pharaoh.

Hathor, the goddess of love and protector of women.

Osiris, the god of the dead, who judges souls in the Underworld.

Anubis, the god of embalming, who watches over the dead.

Hapy, the god of the Nile and provider of the flood.

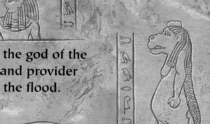

Taweret, the goddess of birth, who looks after mothers and babies.

Bast, the goddess of cats, dancers, and musicians.

Horus, the god whose symbol is a magic eye, which wards off evil spirits.

Thoth, the god of learning and scribe of the gods.

Bes, the protector of homes and families, who scares away evil spirits.

Isis, the wife of Osiris and mother of Horus.

Of course, if you need the help of any of the main gods, you'll have to take an offering for the priests to give to the god on your behalf. But you can keep statues of Bes and Taweret in your own home and pray to them whenever you want to.

MUMMY

Illustrated by ANGUS McBRIDE

ARE YOU DYING to know what goes on inside those mysterious embalming tents? *The Egyptian News* talks to a man who has spent his life preserving dead bodies — the royal embalmer.

❓ Just how important is it to be mummified?

Vital! There's a good chance your soul will overcome the dangers of the journey through the Underworld after you die, but even if it passes all the tests, your soul won't be able to move on to the next world, the Afterlife, if it can't rejoin your body. And how will it do this if your body has rotted away in the meantime?

❓ How do you stop a dead body from rotting?

First, I pull the brain out through the nose. Then I remove the intestines, stomach, lungs, heart, and liver. This has to be done quickly, as these organs rot fast. The smell is awful, so we keep lots of incense burning.

❓ Then what happens to the organs?

The brain is thrown away, but the other organs are preserved with the same mixture that we later use for the body. The heart is placed to the side, as it's put back in the body afterward.

The other four organs are sealed inside stone Canopic jars. Once inside these special containers, the organs are under the protection of the four sons of the god Horus, until the dead person needs them in the Afterlife.

❓ And what happens to the rest of the body?

It's washed in a mixture of juniper-berry oil, palm wine, milk, and spices. Then it's covered in natron salt and left for 40 days.

BOUND UP: Before the body is wrapped, the linen strips are dipped in preserving liquid.

DOC'S SPOT

Illustrated by MAXINE HAMIL & SUE HEAP

THE HEALTH COLUMN in *The Egyptian News* has always been a favorite with our readers. Here's just a small selection of the letters we've received over the years.

But remember, whenever you are ill, go to a doctor — *never* try any of these remedies at home!

What can I do to stop losing my hair?

Ask your doctor for a lotion made from the burned hoof of an ass, the backbone of a rook, and the fat of a black snake. Rub this lotion into your scalp at night.

Don't be put off by the horrible smell — it will scare away the evil spirits that have invaded your head.

I've been suffering from the most terrible headaches. Please help me.

Ask your doctor for a small clay model of a crocodile with green

MAKER

Well for one thing, 40 is a very magical number. And besides, that's how long it takes for the natron to dry the body out.

When the 40 days are up, the body is rubbed with oils and plant resins to soften the skin. Then the body is wrapped in fine linen bandages. This stage can be very time-consuming — it usually takes about 15 days.

❓ **And what happens after those 15 days?**
The mummified body is placed in its coffin and given to the priests for burial, along with the four Canopic jars.

❓ **What do you like most about your job?**
Oh, the challenge! I do everything I can to make people look as lifelike as possible. Sometimes, this can even mean replacing a missing leg or arm with a false one made out of linen or wood.

❓ **As royal embalmer, do you work only for the royal family?**
Nowadays, yes. But anyone can be mummified if they can afford it. Yet watch out for cheap deals—there are some very dishonest embalmers out there. These cheats don't remove the organs, so the body is sure to rot. But you'd never know, as they give you fake Canopic jars made out of solid stone.

❓ **And have you ever embalmed animals?**
Yes, of course. In my time, I've done cobras, lizards, crocodiles — and even scarab beetles.

❓ **What do you think your most difficult job has been so far?**
Definitely the Apis bull. When one of these sacred animals dies, we have to embalm it as lavishly as if it were a pharaoh. But believe me, it takes an awful lot more linen!

eyes. Fill its mouth with grain and repeat the spell the doctor gives you, asking the gods to fight the enemy that's causing the pain inside your head.

This cure is even more effective if you get a scribe to copy the spell onto a piece of linen. Wear this around your head to keep the headache from returning.

How can I protect my wife and children from scorpions?
Simple! In your local temple you'll find a stone slab engraved with a

picture of the hawk god, Horus. Pour some water on the slab, catch it in your hands as it runs off, and then drink it.

Horus will now protect you and your family from the evil spirits of these vile creatures.

My wife is going blind. Can she be cured?
Possibly. Take her to a good doctor, and he will

make an ointment from honey and red earth, mixed together with a ground-up pig's eye.

The doctor will then put this cream in your wife's ears, saying the following spell twice:

"This ointment is for the trouble spot. You will see again."

But don't expect too much — blindness is very difficult to cure.

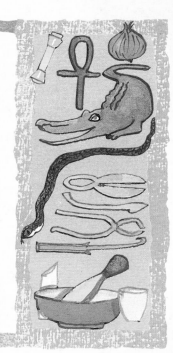

PYRAMID POWER

Illustrated by SIMONE BONI

HARD LABOR: The fine limestone casing is shaped into blocks, ready to be hauled up a steep earth ramp and fitted onto the pyramid.

IT STANDS 482 feet (147 meters) high and contains a staggering 2.3 million blocks of stone. *The Egyptian News* takes a closer look at our most spectacular monument, the Great Pyramid at Giza.

RECORDS FROM the mid-2500s B.C. suggest that during the construction of his huge pyramid tomb, Pharaoh Khufu paid for over 4,000 skilled stone-masons to work on it.

And for three months each year, while the Nile waters flooded the fields, the stonemasons were joined by as many as 100,000 farmers.

Organizing this vast number of workers must have been a daunting responsibility.

Living quarters and workshops had to be specially built. And at least 100,000 bunches of onions and 200,000 loaves of bread had to be found each day to feed the laborers.

The workers' first task was to clear and level an area 756 feet square (70 sq m) for the pyramid base.

While this was being done, 7.2 million tons (6.5 m tons) of stone were collected together at the site.

The pyramid is built mostly of limestone from nearby quarries. But the fine limestone needed for the outer casing had to be ferried across the Nile from the East Bank.

The burial chambers and internal passages are lined with a much harder stone, granite. This was shipped to Giza from the stone quarries at Aswan — a journey of over 500 miles (805 km).

---

50 TONS — WHAT A DRAG

All of the stone blocks are huge and heavy — some weigh over 50 tons (45 m tons)! To move them to the building site, they were eased onto wooden rollers and dragged along by teams of men.

Once the workers had built the basic, stepped-pyramid structure, lime-stone casing blocks were used to fill in the steps.

Level by level, from the top down, the blocks were fitted, chiseled to a flat surface, and then painstakingly polished until they sparkled in the bright sunlight.

The Great Pyramid took thousands of people more than 20 years to complete. And the cost was immense.

Yet standing before it today, who can doubt that Khufu's tomb is one of the greatest wonders in the world!

TOMB TALK

Illustrated by ANGUS M^cBRIDE

SO WHY DID pyramid tombs go out of fashion? *The Egyptian News* talks to a leading architect.

❓ Why are pyramids no longer built?
Too many robbers were breaking into them and stealing the treasure buried with the pharaohs.

❓ Have many of the pyramids been robbed?
Not just many, all! There are more than 80 pyramids in Egypt, and every single one of them has been broken into.

❓ Didn't the architects plan for this?
Of course they did. They designed all kinds of hidden entrances and false passages. A few robbers were tricked and died inside. But sadly, many more succeeded.

❓ Is that why our New Kingdom pharaohs are buried elsewhere?
That's right. Back in the 1500s B.C., the pharaohs decided to go underground — in more ways than one! Their tombs were carved deep into the rocky sides of the Valley of the Kings.

❓ Where is this valley?
It's across the river from Thebes, but I can't tell you the exact location. And it's no good asking any of the tomb builders — they've been sworn to secrecy, too.

❓ But the looting still continues, doesn't it?
Unfortunately, yes. The rock tombs are guarded by security men with dogs, night and day. But even these measures haven't stopped robbers.

❓ Isn't there anything that can be done?
Well, the high priests have now decided on drastic action. Even as we speak, every royal mummy is being moved to a new hiding place — known only to the priesthood.

❓ And will this work?
Only time will tell. ▨

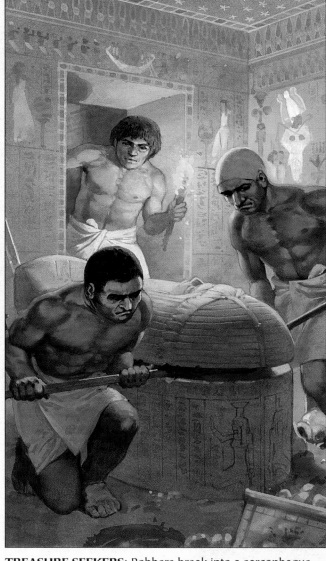

TREASURE SEEKERS: Robbers break into a sarcophagus.

In the 1100s B.C., during the reign of Pharaoh Ramses IX, a number of workmen stood trial for tomb robbing. *The Egyptian News* reprints its report from the first day of the trial.

TOMB ROBBER CONFESSES

THERE WERE dramatic scenes in the city of Thebes today when a gang of workmen was charged with robbing a royal tomb. Our reporter was in court for the trial.

SUCH WAS the severity of the crime that the investigation was led by one of the highest officials in the land, the Vizier of Lower Egypt.

The suspects stood with their heads bowed, as the charges against them were read out.

Forced by mounting evidence to admit to the crime, one of the men suddenly broke down and confessed.

He explained how the gang had forced its way into the tomb and then pried open the stone sarcophagus.

Inside they found the mummy of the pharaoh, encased in three wooden coffins.

The workman's voice trembled as he went on to describe how the coffins were covered in gold and silver and decorated with jewels.

"We took the gold and all the jewels," he admitted, "then we set fire to the coffins."

If the men are found guilty, they will be forced to choose the way in which they will be executed — being burned alive, stabbed, drowned, or beheaded.

The trial continues tomorrow. ▨

BIG AND BEAUTIFUL: Pharaoh Khufu's magnificent funerary boat during the final stages of its construction.

THE LONGEST BOAT

Illustrated by PETER VISSCHER

ONE OF THE BEST examples of our craftsmen's skills is surely Pharaoh Khufu's famous funerary boat. After the pharaoh's death in 2550 B.C., *The Egyptian News* carried this interview with the boat's builder.

❓ Why has this boat become so famous?
Probably because it's the finest boat ever built!

I'm pretty sure it's the longest boat our country has ever seen — it's more than 140 feet (43 m) from prow to stern. That's almost the same as 25 men lying head to toe!

❓ Did it take a long time to build?
Months! There are 1,244 pieces of cedarwood in that boat. And as usual, each piece had to be carved into shape so that all the pieces fitted together perfectly. Then the joints were tightly bound with long strips of leather.

After this, the boat was lowered into the river, where the water made the wood swell so that the joints became tight and waterproof.

Last of all, weeks were spent carving traditional designs into the boat. The prow and the stern were made to look like papyrus reeds, while the walls in the pharaoh's

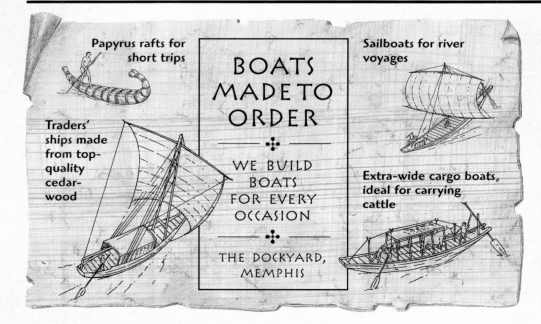

Papyrus rafts for short trips

Traders' ships made from top-quality cedar-wood

BOATS MADE TO ORDER

✦

WE BUILD BOATS FOR EVERY OCCASION

✦

THE DOCKYARD, MEMPHIS

Sailboats for river voyages

Extra-wide cargo boats, ideal for carrying cattle

IN OUR COUNTRY!

cabin were covered with exquisite carvings in the shape of lotus flowers.

❓ It's quite unusual for this much effort to be put into a funerary boat, isn't it?
Well, yes. But then most funerary boats are built simply to be buried with a pharaoh for him to use in the Afterlife.

But Pharaoh Khufu wanted to sail in his boat *before* he died.

And of course, the pharaoh wanted it to be the biggest and grandest boat of all time, just like his magnificent pyramid tomb at Giza!

❓ It must have been upsetting to bury such a fabulous work of art.
I doubt that I'll ever build anything like it again — but that's life, isn't it?

And at least I know that my men were careful when they took the boat apart, before it was buried in the desert next to the pharaoh's pyramid.

Every single piece of wood was labeled so that when Pharaoh Khufu reaches the Afterlife, his servants will know exactly how to put the boat back together again.

❓ Do you think that they'll succeed?
Who knows? But I do like to think that I was responsible for building the boat that will carry our pharaoh on his travels in the Afterlife.

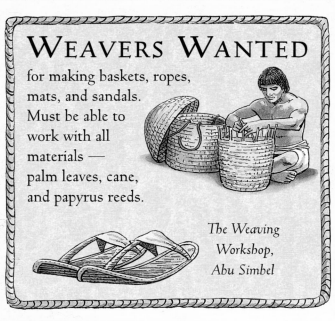

HUNTING CAN KILL

Illustrated by MIKE BOSTOCK

A RECENT STUDY proves what many of us have feared for some time — deaths from hunting accidents are on the increase. *The Egyptian News* examines the risks.

HUNTING has long been our favorite pastime, popular with pharaohs and farmers alike. And when we're not actually out chasing animals, we love to listen to tales of great hunting feats.

How many times have you heard the story about Pharaoh Amenhotep III, who killed 200 lions in his first ten years on the throne? Or how Seti I risked his life by leaping from his chariot to finish off a wounded lion with his lance?

But pride in our skills shouldn't blind us to the dangers of hunting. When Thutmose III was hunting in Syria, his chariot was charged by a wounded elephant. If a soldier hadn't slashed off the elephant's trunk with his sword, the pharaoh's reign would have been brutally cut short!

Of course, pharaohs aren't the only hunters to have narrow escapes.

Countless sportsmen are wounded by other hunters' arrows or by falls from their chariots when chasing gazelles or lions in the desert.

And the marshes of the Nile Delta are so crowded these days that bird catchers have been known to hit one another with their throwing sticks — instead of their prey!

WATCH OUT IN THE WATER

Even fishing on the river can be life-threatening. It's easy to overturn a lightweight raft. And if you fall into the river, drowning isn't your only problem — some parts of the Nile are infested with hungry crocodiles.

But surely the most dangerous sport of all has to be hippo hunting. These enormous, bad-tempered beasts weigh more than 60 men, and their bite can be fatal.

So the next time you're caught up in the thrill of the chase, remember this piece of advice — it may be better to let one get away, so you can live to hunt another day.

BRAVE OR MAD? Hippo hunters go after their prey, armed only with hooked ropes and spears.

FIT FOR LIFE?

WHAT DO YOU like doing when you finish work for the day? Do you head off for a quick swim in the Nile, or would you rather sit under a shady tree and snooze? Try *The Egyptian News*'s quiz to find out just how energetic you really are!

1 It's a scorching hot afternoon, and you've finished your work for the day. *Do you:*
a) Challenge all your friends to a swimming race?
b) Invite them to go on a duck hunt?
c) Ask them over for a drink of fig juice?

2 A lion has been sighted, and it's heading toward your town. *Do you:*
a) Stay inside and bar the doors?
b) Paddle off to safety in a boat?
c) Hire a chariot and go out after it?

3 How do you feel about fishing?
a) Love it! It's great fun, and you get to eat the results.
b) Love it, especially in a well-stocked pond in the garden.
c) Love fish, but prefer to get it at the market.

4 You've been asked to a party where there will be dancing. *Do you:*
a) Practice all the dance steps beforehand to get them just right?
b) Prefer to sit back and watch while other people dance?
c) Like to hop around a bit, but only when you're in the mood?

5 A kind friend has lent you his boat. *Do you:*
a) Rush off to take part in a rowing race?
b) Paddle around in the shallows?
c) Hire a rower and pack a picnic?

ADD UP YOUR POINTS
1 a) 3 points; b) 2 points; c) 1 point
2 a) 1 point; b) 2 points; c) 3 points
3 a) 3 points; b) 2 points; c) 1 point
4 a) 3 points; b) 1 point; c) 2 points
5 a) 3 points; b) 2 points; c) 1 point

HOW DID YOU SCORE?

12–15 points
Well done! You're fighting-fit and full of energy. Keep up the good work.

8–11 points
You seem to have a fair amount of sporting spirit, but you really could make more of an effort. Why don't you take up stick fighting or another sport as a hobby? Or what about going for a run by the Nile?

7 points or fewer
Foreigners might think all Egyptians are lazy by the example you set. Try your best to do our country proud, and get in shape now with an easy sport like swimming.

PERFECT

Illustrated by SUE SHIELDS

The Overseer of the Granaries
of Upper and Lower Egypt
stretches out his arms in generosity.
You are invited to his summer home
to celebrate the feast day of
the cat goddess, Bast.
R.S.V.P. c/o The Pharaoh's Palace, Thebes

YOU'VE been invited to a banquet — and if you're not used to the highlife, the news may fill you with horror! But don't worry, just read on — *The Egyptian News* will tell you how to make the most of the social event of a lifetime....

GETTING READY

① Start with a refreshing all-over wash, then rub yourself from head to toe in scented oils.

WHAT TO WEAR?

④ Don't turn up in the same white linen you wear every day. Dress up for a change!

Men should choose a longer kilt than usual, and women, a tunic with thousands of tiny pleats.

⑤ Get your laundry man to make sure your outfit is spotless. But do remind him to take care when he's by the river. You don't want to lose him or your clothes to the crocodiles!

⑥ Jewelry is a must. Wear a headdress, a necklace, and bangles studded with gems.

AT THE BANQUET

⑧ Prepare for a real meat feast — antelope, gazelle, crane, and heron may all be on the menu.

There'll be figs, grapes, watermelon, and all kinds of delicious pastries, too — so leave room for dessert.

⑨ All meals are sacred to the gods, so show some respect and be on your best behavior.

Laugh only when others do, speak only when spoken to, and don't stare at the other guests.

WHEN THE MEAL IS OVER ...

⑫ Now it's time for the singers and dancers to join the musicians who've been playing all evening.

But remember, as a guest you mustn't get carried away and join in. Stay seated and watch in

PARTYING

2 Now for your face. Mix colored earths with oil yourself, or use ready-made makeup.

A thin black line around the eyes suits men and women alike, as does a deep red lipstick.

3 Buy the best wig of human hair you can afford. Elaborate plaits are very popular.

If you can't afford gems, glass beads are just as colorful. Or tie a bright silk sash around your waist.

And let's not forget the men. A bead collar with a golden falcon-head clasp is all the rage!

7 Ready? Don't forget your best cloak in case it gets chilly later. Now, off you go.

10 After you've eaten, a servant will pour a jug of water over your hands so you can rinse them.

11 And when the perfume cone on your head has melted, call for a serving girl.

She'll bring you a fresh one, along with sweet-smelling flowers to crush between your fingers.

silence while dancers, acrobats, and magicians entertain you for the rest of the evening.

13 Finally, remember there will be plenty to eat and drink, so don't overdo it.

If you do overdo it, ask a servant to bring you a bowl to be sick in. Then you can keep on partying!

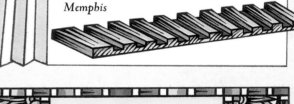

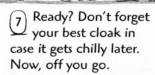
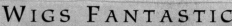

HAPPILY EVER AFTER

Illustrated by SUE SHIELDS

THINK AHEAD: The more children you have now, the more there'll be to look after you in your old age.

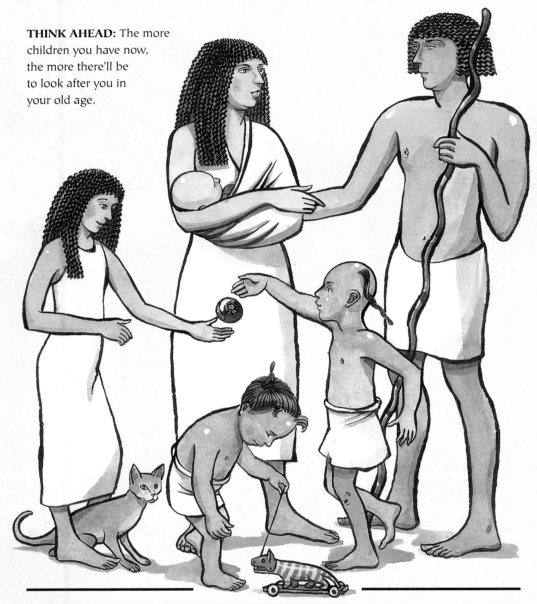

SO YOU'RE about to get married! But are you ready for your new life? *The Egyptian News* answers a young bride-to-be's questions.

❓ When can I move in with my new husband?

Your father has probably sealed all the marriage arrangements already by giving presents to your future husband's father.

So as soon as your new relatives have held the wedding feast, you can move in with them and begin married life.

❓ How can I please my husband most?

Well, you should keep the house clean and tidy and cook delicious meals, of course, just as you do now for your parents. But your most important job will be to have children. Daughters are useful, as they can help you with the housework, but it is vital to have a son.

Not only will a boy help support the family by working for his father, but it is also a son's duty to arrange his parents' funerals. And without a proper ceremony, neither you nor your husband will reach the Afterlife.

❓ But what if I can't have any children?

Don't start worrying yet! How old are you now, 14? And your husband is 20? Well, that's pretty typical these days — you've both got plenty of time ahead of you.

However, if you don't become pregnant after a few years, your husband may want to take a second wife. This doesn't mean that your marriage has to end, though. Lots of women are quite happy to share the work of looking after a home and a family.

❓ Do I really need a marriage contract?

Definitely. Should your husband decide that he wants to divorce you, a contract will make sure that you get about one third of his possessions in a divorce settlement. It will also mean that your husband has to go on supporting you.

Have a note made on the contract of anything you brought with you when you got married, such as a donkey or a bread oven. Then you'll be able to take them with you if you leave. ⌂

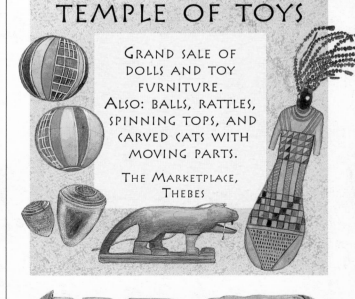

FOOD FOR THOUGHT

LET'S FACE IT—our daily diet of bread, beer, and onions can get a bit boring sometimes. Want to liven things up? Try *The Egyptian News*'s tasty tips.

◎ Brighten up your bread by using barley flour instead of wheat. You'll get a completely different flavor!

◎ Add a spoonful of honey or some aniseed to your bread dough to turn an ordinary loaf into a delicious pastry.

◎ Make any recipe more interesting by adding some garlic. Not only will it greatly improve the flavor of the dish, it also has medicinal properties; and the smell will keep away evil spirits.

◎ When you gut a fish, check whether there are any eggs in its belly. If so, spread them thinly on slices of bread to make a tasty snack or side dish.

◎ Both lentils and chickpeas are filling and very easy to grow. But don't forget to soak them in water overnight before you boil them. A big potful will keep a hungry family fed for days.

◎ Turn a loaf of bread into a delicious honey pastry.

1) Remove the crusts from ten slices of bread, and soak the slices in honey for a half hour.

2) Place the slices, one on top of another, in a deep, lightly greased baking dish.

3) Bake the slices for about 45 minutes. Then chill, slice, and top with heavy cream before serving.

PETS OR PESTS?

Illustrated by PETER DENNIS

ALL CHILDREN long for a pet of their own. But before you give in to their pleas, make sure you've read *The Egyptian News*'s guide to perfect pets.

FOR HUNDREDS of years the most popular pet in our country has been the cat, the beloved symbol of the goddess Bast.

Cats are very useful for keeping the house free of mice and rats. But be warned — when your cat dies, your children may expect you to shave off your eyebrows as a sign of mourning.

They might even ask to visit Bast's temple in the city of Bubastis. Here, for a suitable offering, the priests will mummify your cat and bury it in a special graveyard.

If all that sounds like a bit much, you might think a dog would be easier. But by the time you've traded half your possessions for the latest jeweled dog collar, you'll probably change your mind!

PRETTY MESSY PETS

Gazelles may look pretty, but they are impossible to housetrain, and their horns are dangerous if you have small children.

Pet monkeys are very popular these days — especially with royalty.

But they're always taking things apart to see what's inside, and they'll tear your house to bits in no time. They can also have a nasty bite.

An easier and more practical choice might be some doves. If you build a dovecote near your house, you'll be able to enjoy their gentle cooing all day long.

And when times are hard, and meat is scarce, you can simply pluck one and pop it in the pot!

Of course, even after all our advice, you may still decide to follow fashion and get a feline friend. If you do, please remember — a cat is for life, not just for the festival of Bast.

ANIMAL MAGIC OR MAYHEM? Think carefully before choosing your pet.

LUXURY HOME FOR SALE

Ideal for entertaining — suitable for wealthy government official.

Exquisitely decorated with wall paintings throughout.

Spacious reception and living rooms open onto a large central courtyard with covered walkways and a well-stocked fishpond.

Hallway leads from courtyard to main bedroom, guest rooms, and secluded and comfortable women's rooms. All bedrooms have private bathrooms fitted with a washing slab and sand lavatory.

Fully equipped kitchen includes clay oven and is near to storerooms and servants' quarters.

Box No. 4721

Kitchen

Washing slab and sand lavatory

HOUSES AVAILABLE IN CRAFTWORKERS' VILLAGE

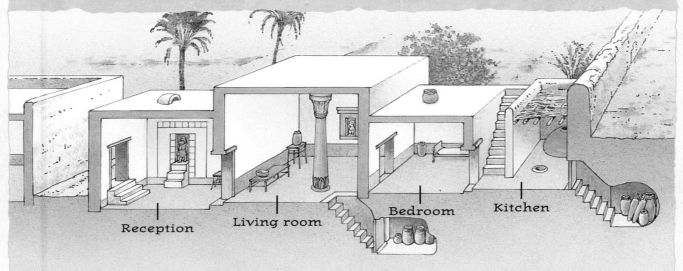

Reception   Living room   Bedroom   Kitchen

Craftworkers needed for royal tombs near Deir el-Medina. Job offers comfortable living quarters in specially built village.

Each house contains a reception room with family altar, a large living room, and one bedroom. Separate kitchen with clay oven has stairway leading to south-facing roof terrace.

Two roomy cellars provide plenty of cool storage space.

Box No. 3256

TOWNHOUSE

Small townhouse in Thebes, ideal for
a young scribe and his family.
Large reception room, two bedrooms
with built-in sleeping platforms,
and underground storage room.
Roof terrace with shady, covered
area for the summer.

Box No. 6920

FARMLAND
AVAILABLE WITH HOUSE

✳

A small plot of farmland near the town
of Abydos has become available — an ideal
opportunity for the son of a farming family.

The house is on the edge of town at the
end of a quiet lane.

There are two rooms on the ground floor
and an outside staircase to a roof
terrace. A small courtyard at the
front of the house contains
a mud-brick oven.

*Apply to the district
governor at
Abydos.*

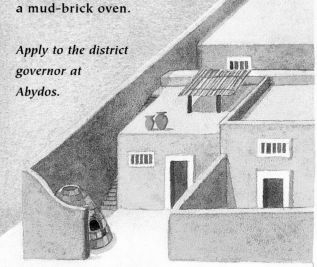

There were three great ages in Egyptian history —
the Old, Middle, and New Kingdoms. Each age
was followed by a period of unrest, civil war, or
invasion known as an Intermediate Period.

◎ **About 5000 B.C.**
The fertile land around
the Nile River becomes
known as Upper Egypt
and Lower Egypt.

◎ **About 3150 B.C.**
These two regions are
united under one ruler.

Hieroglyphs are used for
the first time.

2686–2160 B.C. OLD KINGDOM

◎ **2680 B.C.**
Egypt's first pyramid is
built at Saqqara.

◎ **2550 B.C.**
The Great Pyramid is built
at Giza.

◎ **2160–2040 B.C.**
1st Intermediate Period:
civil war divides Egypt.

2040–1786 B.C. MIDDLE KINGDOM

◎ **2040 B.C.**
Egypt is reunited by
Mentuhotep.

◎ **1786–1550 B.C.**
2nd Intermediate Period:
the Hyksos invaders rule
over Lower Egypt.

1550–1069 B.C. NEW KINGDOM

◎ **1550 B.C.**
After the Hyksos are
driven out, Ahmose I is
crowned pharaoh.

◎ **1479–1457 B.C.**
Queen Hatshepsut reigns
as pharaoh.

◎ **1352–1336 B.C.**
Akhenaton rules Egypt.

◎ **1336–1295 B.C.**
Tutankhamen is pharaoh.
After his death in 1327
B.C., Egypt is ruled by Ay
and then by Horemheb.

◎ **1295–1294 B.C.**
After Horemheb dies, one
of his advisers rules as
Pharaoh Ramses I.

◎ **1291–1258 B.C.**
Egypt is at war with the
Hittites from Asia.

◎ **1279–1213 B.C.**
Ramses II (Ramses the
Great) rules Egypt. In
1258 B.C. he signs a peace
treaty with the Hittites.

◎ **1184–1151 B.C.**
Ramses III reigns. Foreign
armies invade Egypt from
the north and west.

◎ **1151–1069 B.C.**
The next eight pharaohs
to rule Egypt also call
themselves Ramses.

◎ **1069–661 B.C.**
3rd Intermediate Period:
Egypt is divided by civil
war once more.

661–332 B.C. LATE PERIOD

◎ **525–404 B.C.**
Persia invades and takes
control of Egypt.

◎ **404–343 B.C.**
The Persians are defeated
and the country returns to
Egyptian rule.

◎ **343–332 B.C.**
Persia invades again and
regains control of Egypt.

FROM 332 B.C. GREEK-ROMAN PERIOD

◎ **332 B.C.**
Egypt is set free from
Persian rule by Alexander
the Great and becomes
part of his Greek empire.

◎ **305–30 B.C.**
After Alexander's death,
the throne passes to one
of his generals, Ptolemy.
After Ptolemy's death,
Egypt is ruled by his heirs.

◎ **51–30 B.C.**
The last of Ptolemy's
heirs, Cleopatra VII, rules.
She kills herself when
Egypt is conquered by the
Roman Empire.

The dates in this book have the letters B.C. after them.
B.C. stands for "Before Christ" — so 3000 B.C., for
example, means 3,000 years before the birth of Christ.
The ancient Egyptians did not count time in this way.

In this book, many of the place-names are the ones
we use today, such as Cyprus. The ancient Egyptians
would have used different names.

**As the events in this book took place so long
ago, historians cannot be sure of the exact dates.
You may find that the dates we have given vary
a little from those found in other sources.**

For a free color catalog describing Gareth Stevens' list of high-quality books and multimedia programs, call 1-800-542-2595 (USA) or 1-800-461-9120 (Canada). Gareth Stevens Publishing's Fax: (414) 225-0377.

Gareth Stevens Publishing thanks Dr. Phillip Naylor, Director of the Western Civilization Program, Marquette University, Milwaukee, Wisconsin, for his professional help with the information in this book.

Library of Congress Cataloging-in-Publication Data available upon request from publisher. Fax (414) 225-0377 for the attention of the Publishing Records Department.

ISBN 0-8368-2719-8

This edition published in 2000 by
Gareth Stevens Publishing
A World Almanac Education Group Company
1555 North RiverCenter Drive, Suite 201
Milwaukee, Wisconsin 53212 USA

Text © 1997 by Scott Steedman. Illustrations © 1997 by Walker Books Ltd. First U.S. edition published by Candlewick Press, 2067 Massachusetts Ave., Cambridge, MA 02140.

The Egyptian News:
Author: Scott Steedman
Consultant: James Putnam, Egyptologist
Editor: Sarah Hudson
Designer: Beth Aves

Advertisement illustrations by: Nicky Cooney 22br, 23br, 25tr, 30mr, 31tl & bl; Maxine Hamil 15bl, 17tl, 27m & br; Sue Heap 11br, 17bl; Roger Jones 14br; Michaela Stewart 30t; George Thompson 13br, 22tr, 25br, 28br; Peter Visscher 22bl, 30bl; and Mike White 23bl, 27t, 30br.

Decorative borders by: Nicky Cooney 8, 10, 25; Sarah Fox-Davies 1bm; Maxine Hamil 1, 12, 18–19t, 29; Tony Smith 5; and Lesley Redfern 30bl.

With thanks to: B. L. Kearley, Linden Artists Ltd., Linda Rogers Associates, Temple Rogers, Specs Art, Virgil Pomfret Agency

Printed in the United States of America

1 2 3 4 5 6 7 8 9 04 03 02 01 00

FAMOUS PHARAOHS

Zoser	about 2680 B.C.
Khufu	2589–2550 B.C.
Khafre	2550–2532 B.C.
Menkaure	2532–2504 B.C.
Mentuhotep I	2040–1990 B.C.
Hatshepsut	1479–1457 B.C.
Amenhotep III	1390–1352 B.C.
Akhenaton (Amenhotep IV)	1352–1336 B.C.
Tutankhamen	1336–1327 B.C.
Ay	1327–1323 B.C.
Horemheb	1323–1295 B.C.
Seti I	1294–1279 B.C.
Ramses II	1279–1213 B.C.
Ramses III	1184–1153 B.C.
Cleopatra VII	51–30 B.C.